Map of my heart

Samaah Adam

BookLeaf Publishing

Presentation by *BookLeaf Publishing*

Web: www.bookleafpub.com

E-mail: info@bookleafpub.com

ISBN: 9789357211635

First edition 2023

DEDICATION

To the ones I hold close, my family and friends,
I love you all and hope you can continue to
support me.

PREFACE

"I was once young,
I was journeying alone,
and lost my way;
rich I thought myself,
when I met another.
Man is the joy of man."

-Havamal, Stanza 47

Zombie

Wandering
I'm lost and lonely
Searching
I am but a zombie

Orchestrated movements
Yet I trudge along
Would it be better
If I sang a song?

And went trala-lala-la

Yet it's draining
To carry on

I want to keep living
Let it be mindless

Yet nothing is forever
It's brutal
I'm spineless

Luckily

Lucky me

Life is short

So I'll crawl
back up

That seemingly long road ahead

Passionate state of mind

Sickly sweet
Burning heat

At the equator
Now,
But later

Toned down warmth
Coolness brought
forth

But further north

It turns cold,

Bleak

We wish for it to be
over,
again
But it continues

Forever changing
We cannot stay the put
Run, start pacing

One foot

After the other

Two sides, the same coin

I flick that coin
Up into the air
Two futures join
Which will end

Where

To?

To the inevitable.

A shadow is followed
by
Wherever there's light
The morning's swallowed
dry
Spitting out the night

Right?

What is right,
What do I wish for?
The dark pure
Or

The clean white

The future I find
to keep to
The past left behind,
It’s to ultimately remind

Me

To take it all and leave me blind
Or
To resist it all and leave me assigned

To the unknown

Who knows?

Camera

A shot is taken
Captured
A moment in

Time

To face reality

It's an escape
The album
It shows
What I want

Unlike the mirror
I'm faced to come to terms
With myself

I'm alone

Like that camera
A single photo
Cannot do justice

To who I really am

A shot is taken
Captured
A moment in

Time

To face reality

It's an escape
The album
It shows
What I want

Unlike the mirror
I'm faced to come to terms
With myself

I'm alone

Like that camera
A single photo
Cannot do justice

To who I really am

Jigsaw

A lost puzzle piece, out of place
Aimlessly wondering, that dark space

A face?

No...

There's no way out of here
How can I confront
that very same fear?

Wanting to fit in is so dear

To me.

It seems so inane, so asinine
But times up - I'm surrounded on all sides

Am I to abide?

No...

There's only one way for me to escape

As to how I leave this kismet, this fate

Late bloomer

Growing into blossom
No one sees
Sad and solemn
As sturdy as trees

Spring reveals all
New seasons beginning
No longer the fall
But the rise of meaning

Meaning?

To come into play
at a certain time
Immediate or delayed
I'll have my moment to shine

A flower is made

To be seen
It flourishes

There's no such thing as too late

Only a bloom, it now nourishes

Believe it!

To advance down
The path I believe in
I won't fret nor frown
It was always within

Me

That steadfast

Feeling

That I'm alone
It can't go on any longer
So much I've grown
I'll continue to be stronger!

If I were to ever fall;
I'll stand up again
Straight and tall
Realising then

That true strength is:

People who dream
However far it may seem

Just as the moon,
how clouded it can be

Yet appears so large,
shines so bright,
it's light even beams

Yes!

To defy all means
I will continue to achieve

My future still gleams

For the time, being...

To learn of my past and present,
I see a future with you
It may not shine bright
But what I seek, one day, comes true

Where I can look up to the clouds,
That same fateful view
And be glad I'd confided,
Grey skies turn blue

It'll take a while of course,
as long as it had taken

for me
to build up
the courage
to tell you

But in the end it'll be fine,
My message will have gotten through

It's a thing of the past, or so they say

But...

May I present it to you?

And enjoy the future,

The image of mine with yours, so wonderfully true

Blood Orange

When you first entered
I stood there silent
“Why now of all times?”
You came unannounced, uninvited

Inviting

Me into your heart

Everything unravelled
Oh how far I’d travelled
Down the wrong route
Bittersweet, like the grapefruit,

Were your words

Pleasant yet cautioning
Comforting yet advising

Surprising-

My icy front was now comprising
Of nothing

How becoming

I'm becoming
Fond of you
Again

I hope it stays that way then
Like how the sun sets when
The day is over,
again.

The sky fills with warmth
That orange, no more bleeding
New horizons come forth

A new start, that sweet feeling

Brand new

If somebody could point to
The course I should follow
It'd be easy
I'd just be behind you

I'm no longer lost
I've found a direction
You're my compass
My map of perfection

What you aim for
I aim for too
I don't need to look for
The path to sail through

To discover you
Was to discover me
And how glad I am too
As if found lost at sea

See?

Oh how fast anything can be change
But my feelings for you remain
The absolute same

So let’s continue forward
Etching memories into my heart
On your word

Bon voyage!

Pause

I’d love to take a break
But I must keep going
As long as I carry on
I’ve been promised

Something

Out of this world

Oh I’d love to be
The vast expanse
Sky, sun and the sea

Swallowing me whole
Yes, I’d be free
But I can only wish.

To be stuck in time
I’d like to not face
Next time

But it continues…

Anywhere, everywhere

Everywhere I turn
Memories of you burn
Vividly in my mind
I don't have to search to find

You

I wonder
where you are now?

I now
wander

Carelessly in my thoughts

My mind you consume,
and in contemplation
Lingering like perfume
Trying to make reason;
consideration

But there is no explanation.

How can there be?

And in my naivety
I still wish for someone
to see
What you saw in me

Until then I'll keep searching:
Anywhere, everywhere
And I'll stop yearning.

You'll barely be there

You'll never be there

You'll never be anywhere…

Running

I need to leave
That's all that occupies
my mind
I don't care if it's

Lies

Ahead,
The truth exists
I'm out of breath
Survival instincts

Kick in
When I hear you.

Everything is so much
Louder
The shots, it's power
You tower
over me.

I've been found
But you assure me
Reaching a level of calm
But now there's no sound

I can’t hear those words
I’m stuck again

6 feet under

Signal

I must let you know
it's leaving me disoriented
The signals you give out
I'm beginning to grow

Impatient.

I can't read your mind
And vice versa
Let me continue,
not held behind

By the likes of you

Farewell

We'll meet again
By chance of course
Red yellow green
I'll see you then

Shooting star

I wish you were there
To see me shine
I look and stare
You were once mine

To hope and dream about

But now I'm without

You…

As clear as the skies
Has my mind become
I have grown wise,
I no longer succumb

To the persona you drafted,
I was taken for granted,
It lasted

For too long.

Like a meteor shower
You had come and gone
It tasted sour

But it was finally done

The rise of the sun, dawn has

Yet again begun

BPM

My pulse grows louder;
chest tightening
Tugging for its escape
But it's still so frightening

Enlightening

Me

As the past memories blur
Together as one
My speech slurs:

"What have I done?"

The humdrum pace
Begins to seep in
A bit too relaxed
Breathe in

And out

It's so stupid
Yet I resign
I'm not confined;

heart rate flatlines

Crossroads

At a confused point
in my life,
I look both ways

"I'm sorry to disappoint

You"

They're hard to please
it's not my fault

Going through troubles,
to put me at ease

"You were victims of assault,

apologies,
sincerely"

I'll cross those roads
They're nothing to be afraid of,
in comparison.

I reach out filled with love,
both your hands,

as my guidance

Pariah

Left alone
Holding on
To my own

I’m free
But at what cost?
I’ve been disowned

I ask to be anchored
Held down, secure
But what to make of it?
I’m not

Sure

It sounds fun
At first
And now I’m done

The bubble’s been
Burst
Protecting me from

None

Other than my own self

I have to look to her

For guidance, for help

www.ingramcontent.com/pod-product-compliance
Lightning Source LLC
Chambersburg PA
CBHW051750130826
49812CB00033B/1089
* 9 7 8 9 3 5 7 2 1 1 6 3 5 *